Acc 3532   700

This book is to be returned on or before
the last date stamped below.

25 MAR 2000

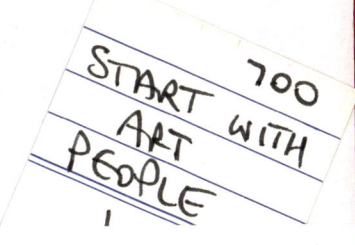

700
START WITH
ART
PEOPLE

ANDREW MARVELL S.H.
SCHOOL LIBRARY
PLEASE RETURN

Start with Art
People

© Aladdin Books Ltd 1999

Designed and produced by
Aladdin Books Ltd
28 Percy Street
London W1P 0LD

ISBN 0-7496-3439-1

First published in Great Britain
in 1999 by
Watts Books
96 Leonard Street
London EC2A 4XD

Project Editor
Sally Hewitt

Editor
Liz White

Design

David West
Children's Book Design

Designer
Flick Killerby

Illustrator
Rob Shone

Picture Research
Carlotta Cooper/Brooks Krikler Research

Printed in Belgium
All rights reserved

A CIP catalogue entry for this book is available from the British Library.

The project editor Sally Hewitt, is an experienced teacher. She writes and edits books for children on a wide variety of subjects including art, science, music and maths.

Sue Lacey is an experienced teacher of art. She currently teaches primary school children in the south of England. In her spare time, she paints and sculpts.

photocredits: Abbreviations: t-top, m-middle, b-bottom, r-right, l-left, c-centre
All the pictures in this book are by Vanessa Bailey apart from the following pages:
Cover br, 4b, 17, 21, 25: AKG London; 4t, 11: AKG. © Succession Picasso/DACS 1999; 8-9b, 13, 27, 29: AKG/Erich Lessing; 14b: Musée Marmottan, Paris; 23: AKG. © DACS 1999; 31: Courtesy of the October Gallery, Paloma.

Start with Art

People

Sue Lacey

FRANKLIN WATTS
LONDON • SYDNEY

INTRODUCTION

Artists work with many different tools and materials to make art. They also spend a great deal of time looking carefully at shapes, patterns and colours in the world around them.

This book is about how artists see **people**. On every page you will find a work of art by a different famous artist, which will give you ideas and inspiration for the project.

You don't have to be a brilliant artist to do the projects. Look at each piece of art, learn about the artists and have fun being creative.

CONTENTS

WORKING LIKE AN ARTIST PAGES 6–7
Learn how to work like a true artist. Use your own sketch book and collect ideas from the world around you.

WALL PAINTING PAGES 8-9
Painting on a surface Paint a picture of your friends or family on a clay surface in the style of the Egyptians.

PICASSO PAGES 10-11
Working in 3-D Picasso sculpted many people. You, too, can make a sculpture of someone you know.

KLIMT PAGES 12-13
Pattern and colour Klimt shows amazingly rich textures and patterns in his work. Make your own collage using many different materials.

MONET PAGES 14-15
Caricatures Monet drew caricatures of his friends and school teachers. You can learn to draw them too.

DEGAS PAGES 16-17
Drawing Degas drew ballet dancers with chalks or pastels. Try using different materials and papers for different effects.

MICHELANGELO PAGES 18-19
Carving Michelangelo carved many images from stone. Try to sculpt an image from a bar of soap.

VAN GOGH PAGES 20-21
Self-portraits Van Gogh used thick paint to create swirls and texture. Paint a self-portrait in the style of Van Gogh.

KLEE PAGES 22-23
Abstract portraits Learn to paint like the abstract painters. Paint a portrait of your family in the style of Paul Klee.

RAVENNA PAGES 24-25
Making a mosaic Glass and stones were used in mosaics in Ravenna. You can make yours from magazines.

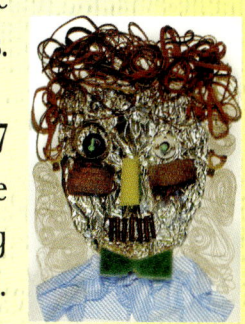

ARCIMBOLDO PAGES 26-27
Assemblage Make a face in the style of Arcimboldo using any strange materials you can find.

MORISOT PAGES 28-29
Use of colour Morisot used colours to create moods. Paint the same image twice using different colours and see the difference.

JEGEDE PAGES 30-31
Imagination Emmanuel Jegede tells stories through his work. Create a work of art that tells a tale of your own.

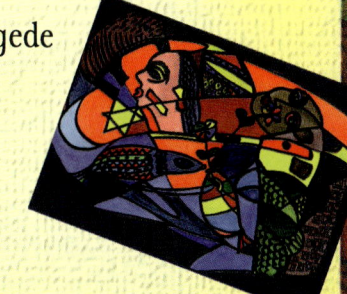

GLOSSARY/INDEX PAGE 32

Working like an artist

It can help you in your work if you start by looking carefully and collecting ideas, just like an artist. Artists usually carry a sketch book round with them all the time so they can get their ideas on paper straight away.

Words
You can write some words to remind you of the shapes, colours and patterns you see.

Materials
Try out different pencils, pens, paints, pastels, crayons and materials to see what they do. Which would be best for this work?

Colour
When using colour, mix all the colours you want first and try them out. It is amazing how many different colours you can make.

Using a sketch book Before you start each project this is the place to put your sketches. Try out your tools and materials, mix colours and stick in some interesting papers and fabrics. You can then choose which you want to use.

Be a magpie

Make a collection of things that are of interest to you like feathers, stones or materials. Anything that catches your eye could be useful in your artwork.

Art box You can collect tools and materials together for your work and put them in a box. Sometimes you may need to go to an art shop to buy exactly what you need. Often you can find things at home you can use. Ask for something for your art box for your birthday.

Drawing people

Drawing people is quite difficult, but with help you can get better at it. Remember always to look carefully.

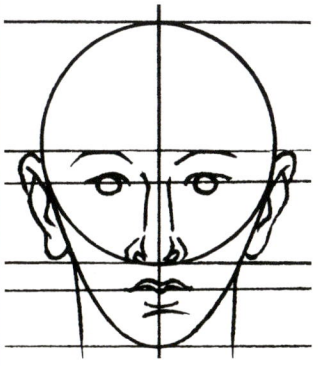

Head shape
Look at the shape and draw the outline. Practise drawing eyes, noses, mouths and ears in your sketch book. How will you do the hair?

Face measurements
It helps when drawing a face to divide the head into sections as shown. See how the eyes sit on one line and the nose on another. Look at where the ears and mouth are.

Body measurements
Remember that about six heads fit into the full-length body. So, whatever size you draw the head, measure two more to the waist and three more to the feet.

Always sketch first and draw in the details afterwards.

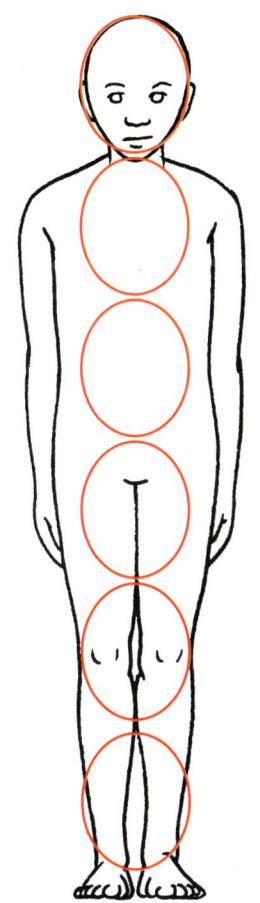

Painting on a Surface

WHAT YOU NEED
Clay • Rolling Pin
Pencils • Paints
Felt-tip Pen

Rekhmere was an Egyptian court official. He wanted his tomb full of pictures of his life. What picture would remind you of home? You could paint a picture of your life on clay. Make sure the people are facing sideways.

Project: Painting on a clay surface

Step 1. Take a lump of clay and knead it with your hands to make it soft.

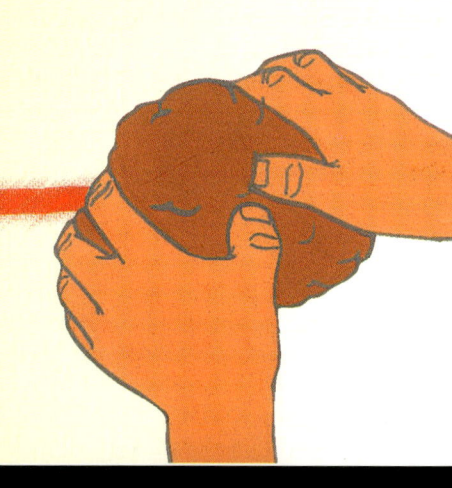

Gallery

Tomb of Rekhmere, Court Official 15th Century BC
Thebes New Kingdom 18th Dynasty

Messages
Messages were put on the wall using word pictures called hieroglyphics, which was Egyptian writing.

Side Views
Look at the people facing sideways. This is how Egyptian artists drew people.

Step 2. Roll out the clay. Don't worry if the edges are not square.

Step 3. While the clay is drying, look at the Egyptian art. When the clay is dry, sketch a picture of you and your family onto it. Make the people face sideways the way they did in Egyptian art.

Step 4. Use paints to colour your clay art. You can darken the outlines with felt-tip pen.

Important ancient Egyptians like Rekhmere used to build their tombs before they died. Artists would paint the walls with wonderful pictures to help make the dead feel at home in the after-life. This painting shows some craftsmen at work carving wood for Rekhmere.

WORKING IN 3-D

WHAT YOU NEED
Balloon • Tape
Cardboard Tube
Flour • Water
Newspaper
Paintbrush • Paints

Sculpture is three-dimensional, or 3-D, which means that it can be looked at from every side. Do some sketches of a friend like Picasso did. You can use your sketches to help you make a papier mâché model to look like your friend.

PROJECT: SCULPTURE OF A HEAD

Step 1. You can make a 3-D head by using a balloon, a tube and some papier mâché. Blow up the balloon and tape it on top of the tube.

Step 2. Mix some flour and water until it is a soggy paste. Tear up newspaper into strips, dip them into the paste and cover the balloon all over with two layers of paper.

Step 3. Make a nose, eyes, ears and mouth by crumpling and moulding newspaper into shapes, and pasting them to the balloon. Don't forget the hair. Now wait for it to dry before you paint it. You could use a bronze colour, or bright colours if you prefer.

Gallery

Head of Dora Maar 1942
PABLO PICASSO (1881 - 1973)

MODELS
Picasso used to ask his friends to sit still for him while he drew them and made sculptures of their heads.

SURFACE
Can you see all the different marks on the face and hair, made by the tools Picasso used?

METHOD
Look at the simple lines and shapes Picasso used to make this sculpture of Dora Maar.

MATERIALS
The head was made in clay first to get all the shapes and details right.

The Spanish artist Pablo Picasso changed the way people saw art because he made unusual and very different paintings, drawings, pottery and sculpture. He did not want his art to look like a photograph. Picasso used his imagination to make art in a way that no one else had ever done.

PATTERN AND COLOUR

WHAT YOU NEED
Card • Tape • Pen
Coloured Tissue
Paper • Sweet
Wrappers
Shiny Paper • Wool
String • Any Fabrics,
Papers or Materials

You can make a figure using patterns and colours. Add some gold and silver paper and paint and make it in the style of Klimt. It would be fun to cover a life-size picture in different fabrics, papers and materials.

PROJECT: A LIFE-SIZED FIGURE

Step 1. Collect pieces of card and tape them together to make them as long as your friend. Draw round your friend with a pen. Use large bits of bright-coloured paper to decorate the background.

Step 2. Look at Klimt's lovely patterns and shapes and copy some. Stick some sweet wrappers or bright fabrics on to make the clothes.

Step 3. Next make the clothing. You can use pictures of faces from magazines for the face. Wool or string will make good hair.

Gallery

The Kiss 1908
GUSTAV KLIMT (1862 - 1918)

Gold
Klimt's father made gold objects. Klimt used to watch him work, and liked to make gold an important part of his own artwork.

Mosaic
After seeing mosaics in Italy, Klimt made this carpet of flowers look like a mosaic.

Model
The woman's face looks like the wife of one of Klimt's close friends.

Pattern
Can you see the different types of pattern on the man's and woman's clothes?

Many people in Austria, where Gustav Klimt lived, thought he was an unusual and interesting artist. He was a big, quiet man who worked hard in his studio from early morning to late evening. All his paintings had a great deal of pattern in them. He used straight lines for men and curved shapes for women. Hands interested him, and he often made them an important part of his pictures.

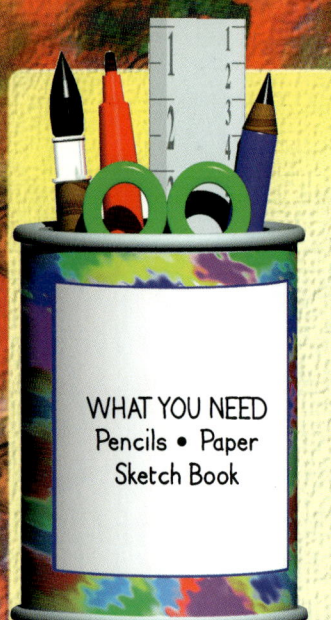

CARICATURES

WHAT YOU NEED
Pencils • Paper
Sketch Book

Drawing was Monet's best subject at school. He found other school work boring, but drew caricatures of his school masters and friends to amuse them. Caricatures will often make fun of famous people, but you can do yours just for enjoyment!

GALLERY

Caricatures c.1855
CLAUDE MONET (1840 - 1926)

CARICATURE
A caricature is made when an artist takes a person's features and exaggerates them.

HEAD AND BODY
Sometimes Monet would give his caricature a small body. This would make the head look even more unusual.

Project: Drawing a Caricature

Step 1. Once you have made your sketch or chosen a photograph, look at it carefully and pick out some special features, like the nose, eyes, hairstyle or chin.

Step 2. Practise enlarging and changing them in your sketch book so they look amusing (but not unkind!)

Claude Monet always enjoyed drawing when he was at school in France. This is when he started to draw caricatures. He also liked to paint out of doors and travelled a great deal, always taking his paints with him. Later, Monet became part of a group of French painters called Impressionists. He wanted to use paint to capture the way light played on landscapes and buildings.

Step 3. Choose what you are going to exaggerate and then draw the caricature. Can you still tell who it is meant to be? You can add a small body like Monet did if you want to.

DRAWING

WHAT YOU NEED
Pastels • Chalks
Charcoals • Pencils
Wax Crayons
Felt Pens • Paper
Scissors
Tracing Paper

Can you see how Degas used pastels to show the movement of the dancers and the light sparkling on their costumes? Degas liked to use different drawing materials in his pictures. You can try using different drawing materials and see what they will do.

PROJECT: MATERIALS

Step 1. Collect as many drawing materials and types of paper as possible. Cut the paper up into squares. Make a viewfinder by folding a piece of paper into four. Cut out the middle and open it out. Pick a dancer from the picture, frame her in your viewfinder and trace over her. Copy her onto the pieces of paper.

Step 2. Try out all your different drawing tools. Which ones make the dancer look the most like the one Degas drew? Stick your drawings onto a piece of dark card to display them.

Gallery

Dancers in Yellow and Green c.1899-1904
EDGAR DEGAS (1834 - 1917)

IMPRESSION
Degas did not show small details on hands and faces. He used pastels to make an impression of them.

DOTS
Dots of yellow make the dancers' costumes come to life and shimmer in the light.

BACKGROUND
Layers of pastels were built up on top of each other to make a lively background. Can you see some of the marks are like scribbles?

STORY
The dancers are all looking at something out of the picture. Perhaps they are waiting for their turn to go on stage.

Edgar Degas was born into a rich family in Paris. He studied art in Paris and Italy and became a very skilled painter. He was one of the first artists to be interested in photography. He looked at people as if he were a camera, drawing them in action rather than posed as for a portrait.

CARVING

WHAT YOU NEED
Plastic Modelling Tools / Nail file
Plastic Knife / Orange Stick
Newspaper
Bar of Soap

Michelangelo used to travel to a quarry to choose pieces of marble for his sculptures. Carvings can be made from many different materials, including soap. It is soft to carve and easy to find at home.

PROJECT: CARVING A SOAP HEAD

Step 1. You will need some plastic modelling tools, but an unwanted nail file, orange stick or plastic knife will do as well. Work on a piece of newspaper so you do not make too much mess.

Step 3. Add the details like eyebrows, hair and cheeks. You could make faces of all your family in different colours, and display them in the bathroom!

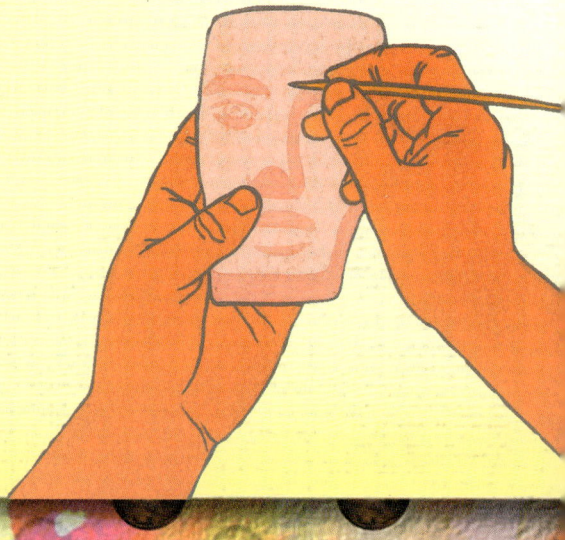

Step 2. Mark out where you will put the eyes, nose, mouth and hair on the soap using a pointed tool. Start to carve out the shapes until the soap looks like a face (see tips on page 7).

GALLERY

The Madonna of the Stairs 1491-2
MICHELANGELO BUONARROTI (1475 - 1564)

MATERIALS
This picture of the Virgin Mary and her baby Jesus was carved from a slab of marble only 5cm thick.

LOW RELIEF
The figures are cut just slightly into the surface of the marble using a fine chisel. This method of working is called low relief.

YOUNG ARTIST
Michelangelo carved this when he was 16. He has made the Virgin Mary and Jesus look like an ordinary mother and baby.

CARVING
Although carved out of solid marble, the clothes flow as if they are real.

By the time he was thirteen, Michelangelo had begun to learn to paint and make sculpture. A great deal of his work was for the Christian church and showed scenes from the Bible. His most famous painting is on the ceiling of the Sistine Chapel in Rome, which he painted all on his own.

Self-Portraits

WHAT YOU NEED
Pencil • Thick Paper
Acrylic Paints
Palette • Brushes
Glue Spreader
Corrugated Card

Look carefully at Van Gogh's self-portrait, then try out some swirls and lines of your own. Mix the paint thickly and put it onto the page using a strip of card or a glue spreader. Get as much texture into your portrait as possible.

Project: Texture

Step 1. Look at yourself in a mirror. Draw your head and shoulders onto some card or thick paper.

Step 2. Start painting, using acrylic paint and a variety of tools. Use a glue spreader, corrugated card and brushes. You can even squeeze the paint straight from the tube! Make the paint really thick.

Step 3. Add swirls of paint in different colours, building up the texture. You can add more detail to your painting once the thick paint has dried a bit. You now have a portrait of yourself in the style of Van Gogh.

Gallery

Self-Portrait 1889
Vincent Van Gogh (1853-1890)

Shading
To show light and dark on the painting, Van Gogh used shades of blue and green.

Colour
You can see that a mixture of blues, greens and white have been used in this picture. Van Gogh chose colours to fit his mood. How do you think he was feeling?

Brush Strokes
Look closely at the background and you will see a swirly pattern. There are also curved and straight lines on Van Gogh's jacket and face.

Thick Paint
Van Gogh used very thick oil paint. He would put it on the canvas with big brush strokes.

Vincent Van Gogh grew up in Holland, but later lived and worked on his paintings in France. When he was 36, he painted this portrait of himself looking like a French farmer. Vincent did not want to paint like anyone else and nobody seemed to understand his way of working.

ABSTRACT PORTRAITS

WHAT YOU NEED
Paper • Pens
Pencils • Ruler
Crayons • Chalks
Paints

Paul Klee's painting is abstract rather than realistic. He used geometric shapes like circles, ovals, triangles, rectangles and squares to make his portrait. You can draw a picture of people you know in the same style.

PROJECT: ARRANGING SHAPES

Step 1. Look at what you are going to draw and decide how you could divide it into geometric shapes. Draw in the body and head shapes as a starting point.

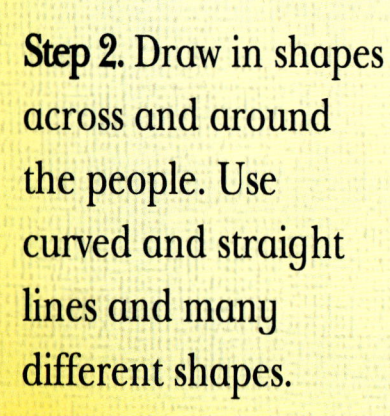

Step 2. Draw in shapes across and around the people. Use curved and straight lines and many different shapes.

Step 3. Choose some colours that you think will give the portraits life and character. You can use pencils, crayons, chalks or paints to shade in your drawing.

Gallery

Senecio 1922
PAUL KLEE (1879 - 1940)

SIMPLE SHAPES
Can you see how this face is made up of simple rectangles, squares, triangles and circles?

COLOUR
Each shape and colour is carefully chosen to give the face expression and make it come alive.

TEXTURE
Klee painted this picture on linen, which is a roughly woven material. You can see the texture of the cloth through the paint.

Paul Klee did not paint like other artists of his day. He liked to work alone and usually did about 200 pictures a year, each one different from the last. Many of his pictures were made up of shapes and patterns that had a hidden meaning. This portrait is called Senecio, which is the name of a group of plants. The title is the clue to help us see that Klee has painted this face to look rather like the head of a flower.

Making a Mosaic

WHAT YOU NEED
Magazines • Pencil
Card • Photograph
to Copy • Glue
Brush • PVA Glue

Look at the colours, patterns and tones in this mosaic from Ravenna in Italy. It was made by pressing pieces of coloured glass, marble and stone into cement to make a large picture. You can make your own mosaic using paper.

Project: Mosaic portrait

Step 1. Find a picture in a magazine or a photo of a friend. Draw an outline of the face onto some card.

Step 2. Cut or tear lots of coloured scraps of paper from magazines. Choose colours that you can use to create a face, mouth, eyes, nose and hair. Try to find lots of different tones of the same colour.

Step 3. Glue the scraps onto the card to build up the face. When it is dry, paint over it with PVA glue mixed with some water as a varnish.

Gallery

The Empress Theodora with Her Retinue c.547
Ravenna, Italy

Colour
Look at the wonderfully rich colours used for this mosaic. Small pieces of bright glass were the main material used.

Materials
Semi-precious stones were used in the mosaic to make Empress Theodora's beautiful jewellery.

Detail
Many pieces were used to create each face. They are so well done that from a distance they look like a painting.

Patterns
How many different patterns are there? They show how important she was.

This mosaic is almost 1,500 years old. Many churches used mosaics to tell Bible stories. The artist for this mosaic is unknown but the mosaics in Ravenna are probably the most famous in the world. This one shows the Roman Empress Theodora bringing gifts to the church.

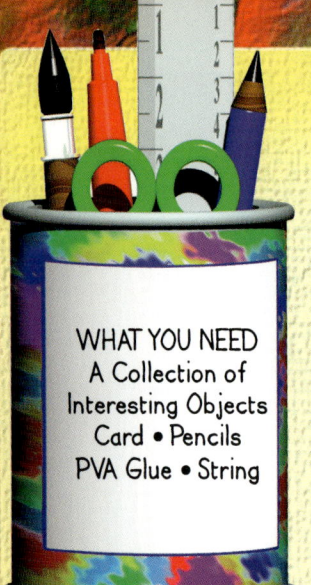

Assemblage

WHAT YOU NEED
A Collection of Interesting Objects
Card • Pencils
PVA Glue • String

Many famous people liked Arcimboldo's portraits so much that they paid him to paint one for them. Arcimboldo's paintings are made by assembling a collection of objects. You can make a strange head using things you have at home.

Project: Collage

Step 1. Collect all kinds of interesting objects like paper clips, cotton reels, string, nuts and bolts, hooks, screws, pins, wire, wrappers and wood. Find a piece of card from an old box. It will need to be thick and fairly big. Glue on some fine string to make the outline of a face and neck.

Step 2. Try out different objects you have collected to see which look best as eyes, ears, nose and mouth. Choose something that would make good hair. When you have made your arrangement, stick it down with strong glue and leave it to dry. You could frame it and invite your friends to see your curious picture.

26

GALLERY

Vertumnus 1590
GIUSEPPE ARCIMBOLDO (1527 - 1593)

FRUIT
Can you see why each piece of fruit has been chosen? The pear looks like the shape of a nose.

MATERIALS
What would you choose to make a head, eyes, nose, mouth and hair if you were to make a picture like Arcimboldo's?

DETAIL
Each fruit and flower is painted with great care, showing every detail. Some look good enough to eat.

SUBJECT
Do you find this man's head interesting, friendly or a bit frightening?

An Italian, born in 1527, Arcimboldo started his work as an artist by making stained-glass windows for churches. He became interested in painting strange and curious people who were considered grotesque. He painted fruit, flowers, trees and vegetables to create his amazing heads.

USE OF COLOUR

WHAT YOU NEED
Paper • Pencil
Tracing Paper
Paints
Paintbrush

Berthe Morisot used cool colours to create a peaceful mood. In your sketch book try mixing warm reds, yellows, purples and oranges as well as cool greens, blues, greys and mauves. You can use them to create different moods in your work.

PROJECT: WARM AND COOL COLOURS

Step 1. Draw a picture of something you enjoy doing. Trace over it and make an exact copy onto a piece of paper the same size. Paint one picture using only warm colours.

Step 2. Paint the second picture using only cool colours and see how different the two pictures look. How do the colours make you feel? Which one do you prefer?

Gallery

The Cradle 1872
BERTHE MORISOT (1841 - 1895)

SHADING
The woman is Edma, Berthe's sister. The loving mother with her black hair and dark clothes, quietly looking at her baby asleep, draws your eye towards the baby in the cradle.

COLOURS
Most of the colours used by Morisot are cool blues, greys, greens and whites. They create a sense of peace and quiet, just right for the baby.

LIGHT
The dark background makes the light cradle stand out.

Women were not allowed to study art at college when Berthe Morisot lived in France. Berthe and her sister Edma were determined to learn to paint, so their father allowed them to have lessons. Berthe had a free and easy style, putting the paint on the canvas so you could see the different brush strokes and colours.

IMAGINATION

WHAT YOU NEED
Pencil • White Card
Felt-tip Pen • Paints

Emmanuel Taiwo Jegede's paintings tell a story about his life and the family and friends he has known in Africa and England. You can make your own picture that tells a story – just let your pencil do the work.

PROJECT: STORYTELLING

Step 1. Use a pencil to make a pattern on a piece of white card. Imagine you are young again and cannot write or draw.

Step 2. Now look at your pattern. Can you see your pet dog, fish or cat? Can you find a house, tree or bird shape? Fill in any shapes with a pen.

Step 3. You can follow some of the scribble lines to make more shapes. Use paint or felt pens to fill in the pictures and patterns you have drawn using lots of bright colours.

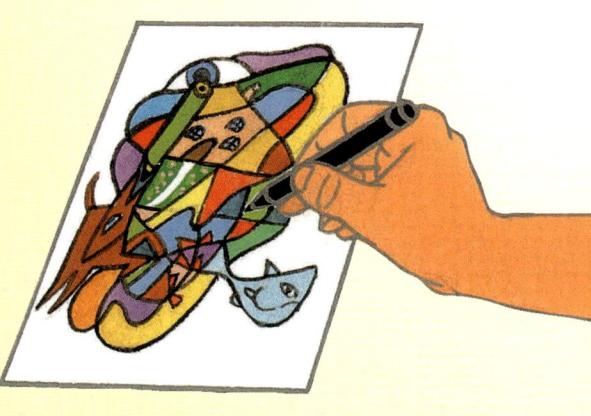

Step 4. Use a black felt pen to add some patterns to some of the shapes. You now have a picture about you and parts of your life.

Gallery

Path of Joy 1993
EMMANUEL TAIWO JEGEDE (1943 -)

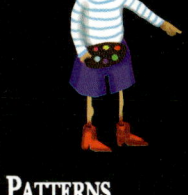

PATTERNS
How many different patterns has Emmanuel used to decorate his picture?

FACES
Can you imagine who all these people are on the Path of Joy? Perhaps they are all the people Emmanuel knows.

COLOURS
This is a picture about joy, so the colours Emmanuel has used are bright and cheerful.

HANDS
The hands in the picture are many different colours, showing different people happy together.

In the village in Nigeria, Africa, where Emmanuel Jegede was born, artists are highly thought of. An artist would also write poetry and make music. Jegede studied sculpture and art in Nigeria, but then went to England. He writes beautiful poetry, teaches art to people of all ages and paints colourful pictures.

GLOSSARY

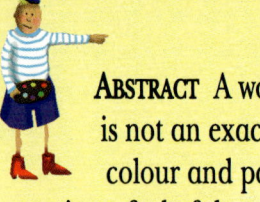

ABSTRACT A work of art that is not an exact copy. Shape, colour and pattern are used to give a feel of the subject.

ASSEMBLAGE A work of art made up of a collection of selected objects.

CANVAS Thick cotton or linen material stretched over a wooden frame, used instead of paper for painting on.

CARICATURE Comic picture of a person made by drawing a larger chin, nose, eyes and hair with a smaller body.

CARVING Making a shape, pattern or design out of material like wood or stone by cutting with a sharp tool.

COLLAGE Placing different materials onto a backing to make a pattern or picture.

GROTESQUE A face or design that is made to look comically strange.

IMPRESSIONISTS A group of French artists who painted the first impression of what they were looking at.

MARBLE Hard rock that comes in many patterns and colours and can be cut, carved and polished.

MOSAIC A picture made on a wall or floor by pressing glass and stones into cement.

PORTRAIT A picture of a person or people that can be made using any materials.

RELIEF A carving made on the surface of a piece of rock, stone or wood.

SCULPTURE Making shapes from hard or soft materials, to make a person, animal or design that can be looked at from all sides.

SHADE A darker or lighter tone of the same colour used to make a picture have more depth.

INDEX

A
abstract 22, 32
assemblage 26, 27, 32

C
canvas 21, 32
caricature 14, 15, 32
carving 18, 19, 32
clay 8, 9, 11
collage 26, 32
crayons 16, 22

G
grotesque 27, 32

H
hieroglyphics 8

I
imagination 30, 31
Impressionists 15, 17, 32

L
low relief 19

M
marble 18, 19, 24, 32
mosaic 13, 24, 25, 32

P
papier mâché 10
pastels 16, 17
portraits 20, 21, 26, 27, 32

R
relief 19, 32

S
sculpture 10, 11, 18, 19, 31, 32
shade 29, 32
shapes 22, 23